MW01119377

CHRISTOPHER
COLUMBUS

Please visit our web site at: www.worldalmanaclibrary.com
For a free color catalog describing World Almanac® Library's list of high-quality books
and multimedia programs, call 1-800-848-2928 (USA) or 1-800-387-3178 (Canada).
World Almanac® Library's fax: (414) 332-3567.

Library of Congress Cataloging-in-Publication Data

Nathan, Melissa.
    Christopher Columbus / by Melissa Nathan.
       p. cm. — (Great explorers)
    Includes bibliographical references and index.
    Summary: Describes the life of explorer Christopher Columbus and discusses his voyages to the islands
now known as the West Indies.
      ISBN 0-8368-5013-0 (lib. bdg.)
      ISBN 0-8368-5173-0 (softcover)
      1. Columbus, Christopher—Juvenile literature. 2. Explorers—America—Biography—Juvenile literature.
3. Explorers—Spain—Biography—Juvenile literature. 4. America—Discovery and exploration—Spanish—
Juvenile literature. [1. Columbus, Christopher. 2. Explorers. 3. America—Discovery and exploration—
Spanish.] I. Title. II. Great explorers (Milwaukee, Wis.)
    E111.N36   2002
    970.01'5'092—dc21
    [B]   2003043095

This North American edition first published in 2004 by
World Almanac® Library
330 West Olive Street, Suite 100
Milwaukee, Wisconsin 53212 USA

This U.S. edition copyright © 2004 by World Almanac® Library.
Created with original © 2001 by Quartz Editions,
112 Station Road, Edgware HA8 7AQ, U.K.
Additional end matter copyright © 2004 by World Almanac® Library.

Series Editor: Tamara Green
World Almanac® Library editor: JoAnn Early Macken
World Almanac® Library designer: Melissa Valuch

The creators and publishers of this volume wish to thank the following for their kind permission to feature
illustration material:
Front cover: main image, Helen Jones/other images (from top to bottom) The Art Archive/AKG /AKG/Naval
Museum, Pegli/AKG/Mary Evans Picture Library
Back cover: (from top to bottom) Mary Evans Picture Library/Mary Evans Picture Library/AKG/AKG/AKG
5 t Naval Museum, Pegli/b AKG; 6 Mary Evans Picture Library c The Art Archive; 7 Helen Jones; 8 t Ancient Art
& Architecture Collection/c, b Mary Evans Picture Library; 10 t Ancient Art & Architecture Collection/c Mary
Evans Picture Library/b AKG; 11 t AKG/c The Art Archive; 12-13 Stuart Brendon; 14 t Bridgeman Art Library/b
AKG; 16 t Mary Evans Picture Library/b AKG; 17 t National Maritime Museum, Greenwich/b AKG;
18 t Bridgeman Art Library/b Mary Evans Picture Library; 19 t, b The Art Archive; 20 t Ancient Art &
Architecture Collection/b Bridgeman Art Library, Salvador Dali Museum, Florida; 21 t NHPA, D. Heuclin/b
NHPA, B. Coster; 22 t, c Bridgeman Art Library/b Mary Evans Picture Library; 23 AKG; 24 t Bridgeman Art
Library/c, b Mary Evans Picture Library; 25 t Mary Evans Picture Library/b AKG; 26 t, b AKG; 27 t, b Mary
Evans Picture Library; 28 t NHPA, D. Heuclin/c AKG/b Mary Evans Picture Library; 30 t Mary Evans Picture
Library/b AKG; 31 t AKG; 32 t, b AKG/c The Art Archive; 33 t Bridgeman Art Library/c, b Mary Evans Picture
Library; 34 t, c Bridgeman Art Library/b AKG; 35 t Bridgeman Art Library/c AKG/b Oxford Scientific Films, E.
Parker; 36 t, c, b Bridgeman Art Library; 38 t Bridgeman Art Library/b The Houghton Library, Harvard
University; 39 t Harvard University/b The Art Archive; 40 t The Art Archive, Mireille Vautier/c, b Bridgeman Art
Library; 42 t Bridgeman Art Library/b AKG; 43 Helen Jones

Printed in Canada

1 2 3 4 5 6 7 8 9 07 06 05 04 03

CHRISTOPHER COLUMBUS

MELISSA NATHAN

WORLD ALMANAC® LIBRARY

CONTENTS

INTRODUCTION

CHRISTOPHER COLUMBUS made four exploratory voyages from Spain to what became known as the New World. Each time he believed he had reached Asia.

This was the coat of arms of Columbus, who won the title of "Admiral of the Ocean Seas."

It comes as a complete surprise to many people to learn that the discovery of the mainland of North America should not be attributed to Columbus. But does this make him any less of a great explorer? Where did he sail to? And what were his achievements? The true story unfolds within the pages of this highly illustrated book.

Near-fatal shipwrecks, lucky escapes, encounters with unfamiliar Native peoples and new forms of wildlife, imprisonment, the search for gold — all featured in the life of this extraordinary adventurer.

Known as Cristoforo Colombo in Italy and Cristobal Colon in Spain, Columbus has been claimed by many other countries — Corsica, Germany, Greece, and Armenia among them — as a former citizen, proving how highly regarded this fifteenth-century explorer has become over the centuries. But was he a heroic sea captain and an honorable man? Or should he be criticized for his conduct toward his crew and the Native peoples he encountered?

Columbus did not succeed in finding a westerly route to the Orient. Although he explored many lands in and around the Caribbean Sea, he never reached the shores of North America. On behalf of his sponsors, King Ferdinand and Queen Isabella, Columbus claimed the lands he explored for Spain.

In spite of his faults, Columbus made major contributions to a greater understanding of our planet's geography.

CHRISTOPHER COLUMBUS

IN SEARCH OF GLORY

The illustration above depicts in symbolic form Christopher Columbus's main achievements as a fifteenth-century explorer.

Columbus changed Europe's view of the world after he set sail for what eventually became known as the New World in 1492, hoping to find gold and spices.

Christopher Columbus was the eldest son in a family of weavers from Genoa, Italy, a thriving seaport that was a major hub of international trade in the fifteenth century. He was born at an exciting time in world history, the age of the Renaissance, an era when interest in art, philosophy, and exploration was at a height. It took perseverance and driving ambition for him to rise from modest origins and become one of the greatest explorers of all time.

This painting shows ships at the busy Italian port of Genoa, where Columbus spent his early childhood.

While he was governor, Columbus lived in La Navidad on the Caribbean island of Hispaniola in an impressive villa like this one (*right*).

> " *I presented [to Spain] the Indies . . .*
> *I gave them, as a thing that was mine.* "
>
> FROM COLUMBUS'S WILL

According to a biography written by his son, Ferdinand, Columbus studied astronomy, geography, and cosmology as a young man. He claimed to come from distinguished ancestors. According to some historians, however, it is more likely that Columbus's father, Domenico, never rose beyond the lower middle classes and had a constant struggle to make ends meet.

Columbus had a younger brother, Bartholomew, who became his closest friend and sailed with him to the West Indies, along with another brother, Giacamo, who later became known as Diego.

In 1479, Columbus settled in Lisbon, Portugal. Two years later, he married Felipa Perestrello Moniz, a noblewoman. Her high rank, however, did not bring a substantial dowry with it. In 1480, their son Diego was born. Soon after that, Felipa died. Before Diego was five, Columbus moved again, to Castile, an area that is now part of Spain.

No fifteenth-century portrait of Columbus has ever been found. The facial features in this new painting were based on a description of him written by his second son, Ferdinand.

This stone cross, overlooking a modern settlement on the island of Santa María in the Azores, was erected to commemorate Columbus's landing there.

Columbus had to handle his crew with care so they did not mutiny. This image shows him trying to calm his anxious men during one of the many storms they faced.

Here, Columbus met Beatriz Enriquez de Harana, with whom he had a second child, Ferdinand.

PORTRAIT OF A SAILOR

No contemporary paintings of Columbus exist, but according to an early biographer, he had long hair and an untidy beard, and his eyes were quick to show anger. His son Ferdinand wrote of him, "The Admiral was a well-built man of more than average height. His face was long, with rather high cheekbones.

A welcome awaited Columbus when he returned to Castile after his first voyage. He rode on horseback through the streets of Barcelona as the crowds cheered.

"His person was neither fat nor thin. His nose was aquiline, his eyes light; his complexion was also light with a ruddy tinge. In his youth his hair was fair, but it turned white in his thirties."

EARLY DAYS AT SEA

Records show that at the age of fourteen, Columbus worked as a ship's agent for a wealthy family. Not until 1471, when he was in his early twenties, was there a mention of an actual voyage — to the island of Chios in the Aegean Sea, off the coast of Greece. While still a young man, Columbus sailed right around the Mediterranean coast. He also signed up for longer voyages. By the time he was twenty-six, he had been as far south as the island of Madeira. He is also known to have sailed as far north as Iceland. But it was not just exploration and the discovery of new lands that fascinated Columbus.

Throughout his life, he remained a devoted Christian and obeyed the request of his royal sponsors that if he discovered new lands, he should try to convert the inhabitants to this faith. His religious fervor was so strong that he saw himself as an instrument of God and believed the Almighty had given him a specific task.

The New World is that part of the globe – most specifically the American continents and islands in the Caribbean — that, before the end of the fifteenth century, had not yet been discovered and fully mapped by Europeans or other explorers from elsewhere in the world.

At the start of his career, however, Columbus faced widespread mockery in Italy and Castile because of his revolutionary beliefs about the size of the world.

> ❝ *Noble gentlemen, although my body is here [in Seville], my heart is always there [in Genoa].*
>
> FROM COLUMBUS'S LETTER TO THE BANK OF ST. GEORGE, GENOA ❞

Columbus had so much self-confidence that each time he faced rejection, it made him more determined. This quality should have made Columbus a fine leader, but he was not. He had constant problems with his crew. On his first voyage, for example, he is said to have offered ten thousand gold coins to whoever saw land first. At 2 A.M. on October 12, 1492, a sailor named Rodrigo de Triana cried, "Land Ahoy!" and was declared the winner. Later, Columbus said he had seen the shore many hours previously and claimed the prize himself. No one, however, suffered as much at the hands of Columbus as the Native people of the lands he explored.

ITALIAN PATRIOT

Although Columbus's expeditions were financed by Castilian royalty, he remained fond of his country of birth, Italy, and of his native town in particular. In fact, he left orders for his son Diego to establish a fund for Genoa's poor after his death.

Some historians say Columbus was a genius. Others, however, brand him a religious fanatic. As you follow his fascinating adventures, you are sure to find out more about what motivated him. This will help you assess for yourself whether, from a twenty-first-century standpoint, he deserves universal acclaim or condemnation.

TIME LINE

1451
Columbus is born in Genoa, Italy. Many years later, he settles in Portugal.

1486
Columbus meets the king and queen of Castile for the first time.

1492-1494
Columbus sets sail and lands on San Salvador, later exploring the island of Cuba and reaching Hispaniola. The *Santa María* is wrecked. In 1493, he returns to Spain. He sails again in 1494.

1496
Columbus returns to Castile to defend himself against charges of misgovernment on Hispaniola.

1498
Columbus sails for a third time, to Trinidad.

1500
Columbus is arrested and returns to Spain as a prisoner in chains.

1502
Columbus embarks on a final voyage. He is marooned on Jamaica and waits to be rescued.

1506
Columbus dies, rich but embittered.

Excited sailors onboard the *Pinta* (*above*) are shown as they sight land after a lengthy voyage.

SAILING TO THE WEST

Inspired by the writings of Marco Polo, Columbus intended to sail to the Orient to find gold, spices, and precious stones. Why did he take a westerly route?

Columbus was undoubtedly something of a visionary, but he was not the only man of his era who was interested in reaching the East. Contrary to popular opinion of the time, however, he believed such a speedy route might lie due west.

As it happened, he was wrong. He made his big mistake by using Roman rather than Arabic miles when studying an existing chart of the oceans.

This error gave him the impression that the waters he intended to cross, which he thought lay between Spain and India, were very narrow — a hugely appealing idea for any sailor who was hungry for riches. What neither he nor any other European knew at the time, however, was that the vast continents of North and South America in the middle of these waters completely blocked his way.

This 1494 woodcut shows Columbus sailing in Caribbean waters near Hispaniola.

Bartholomew Columbus, who sailed with his more famous brother, produced this map. Note the positions of Asia and Mondo Novo, or the New World.

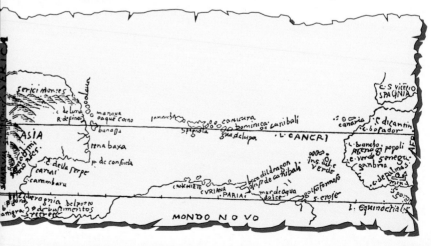

Columbus was wise enough to know that the world was round. He was not alone in this, although many people still thought it was flat. Some uneducated people even feared Columbus planned to sail off the map and over the edge of the world.

A CHANGE OF VIEW

Columbus actually changed his mind on his third voyage, when he landed on the South American continent for the first time.

This region seemed truly to be part of another realm. Columbus's only explanation was that the world was not round after all but irregular in shape. He wrote: "I have come to another conclusion respecting the earth, namely, that it is not round as they describe, but of the form of a pear . . . or like a round ball, upon one part of which is a prominence."

A chart on pages 12-13 shows the likely routes Columbus took for each of his voyages, the places where his ships landed, and the seas they sailed.

MAKING HEADWAY

POINT OF DEPARTURE

The Castilian port of Palos was chosen as the point of departure for Columbus's fleet. Both Cádiz and Seville had been rejected. They were thought too busy with the forced emigration of Spanish Jews following the Inquisition of 1492. Ferdinand and Isabella were also eager to keep costs down and remembered that Palos was in debt to them. A royal decree read, "Because of your crimes . . . you were sentenced to supply two caravels, equipped at your expense, for twelve months, whenever we require them. . . .

"We command that within ten days of receiving this letter, you have ready two equipped caravels . . . to depart with the said Christopher Columbus whither we have commanded him to go."

The port of Palos obeyed, providing both the *Pinta* and the smaller *Niña*. A third ship, the *Gallega*, was chartered by Columbus and renamed the *Santa María*. Because of its size, this nao became the flagship of the fleet. The three ships are shown leaving Palos, (*left*) and together at sea (*below*).

CHOICE OF CREW

The King and Queen of Castile also tried to assist with appointing an adequate number for Columbus's crew by granting a pardon to anyone on trial in a court of law if he agreed to sign on. Finally, though, only four men took advantage of the amnesty.

Many more were clearly needed. A wealthy shipowner from Palos, Martin Alonso Pinzón, agreed to captain the *Pinta*. To this day, he remains highly regarded in Palos, and Pinzón Day is celebrated there every year on March 15. Columbus's brother and his cousin also served on the *Pinta*. Pinzón's brother Vicente Yanez Pinzón captained the *Niña*. Many years later, a sailor from Palos wrote, "Martin Alonso put much zeal into enlisting and encouraging crewmen as though the discovery was to be for his children's sakes."

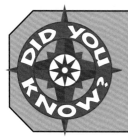

An Italian scholar, Paolo Tosconelli, first gave Christopher Columbus the false idea that there might be a speedy westerly sea route to Cathay (China) from Europe. Columbus also gained the erroneous impression that this planet is a lot smaller than it actually is.

NORTH AMERICA

FROM THE NEW WORLD

Among the finds that were introduced to Europeans as a result of Columbus's four expeditions were several new types of edible plants. Among them were something described as a turniplike root in a variety of shapes, from which the local West Indian people made their staple diet, a sort of bread that would remain fresh for several days. First, poison had to be removed from the roots. Pineapples were also new to Europeans and described as "like artichokes but four times as tall . . . and shaped like a pine cone."

Columbus seems to have been impressed by the well-kept West Indian houses, which he described as arranged haphazardly and made of beautiful palm branches.

The natives boasted of oysters yielding fine pearls, but Columbus did not find any. Corn, first found growing on Caribbean islands, is of course now common worldwide. Most curious of all to Columbus and other Europeans was the smoking of tobacco for both social and religious purposes.

GULF OF MEXICO

CENTRAL AMERICA

Chances are that Columbus possessed a globe on which the places discovered by Europeans by that time were marked. To these, he probably added the new lands he had found as he plotted his course. This map shows the likely route of each of his four voyages. On none of these expeditions did he reach the mainland of North America.

THE VOYAGES OF COLUMBUS

BAHAMAS

ATLANTIC OCEAN

CUBA

HISPANIOLA

PUERTO RICO

JAMAICA

W E S T I N D I E S

Guadeloupe

St. Lucia

HONDURAS

CARIBBEAN SEA

NICARAGUA

Tobago

Trinidad

COSTA RICA

PANAMA

VENEZUELA

S O U T H A M E R I C A

KEY

———	1st Voyage 1492-1493
———	2nd Voyage 1493-1496
———	3rd Voyage 1498
———	4th Voyage 1502-1503

LIFE ONBOARD SHIP

Inaccurate charts, filthy conditions, and crowded sleeping arrangements were just some of the discomforts and difficulties Columbus and his crew faced.

The ships of Columbus's fleet had many more features than the West Indians' simple dugout canoes. Yet conditions onboard fifteenth-century European vessels were far from ideal.

This map, originally sketched by Columbus himself (*below*), shows the coastline of Hispaniola and the smaller offshore island of La Tortuga.

On present-day voyages, using twenty-first-century navigational techniques, a crew can determine without any problem the precise direction in which they are traveling, their speed, and the distance covered. For fifteenth-century sailors, however, it was an entirely different matter. They were restricted, for example, to the use of charts that were often wildly inaccurate.

To keep track of time, a page turned an hourglass (and might even have speeded things up in an attempt to finish his watch a little earlier). There would also have been a basic compass, a relatively recent import from China that required knowledge of the relationship between true north, magnetic north, and the polestar, or North Star (skills far beyond the average mariner of the time); a quadrant; and an astrolabe. Both the quadrant and the astrolabe were fine on firm ground but often worse than useless on heaving seas. Columbus's crew was said to so distrust the astrolabe that they secretly plotted to throw him overboard when they saw him using one.

DID YOU KNOW?

In the fifteenth century, many sailors believed in mermaids. In his log, Columbus recorded sighting three of them. It is now considered likely, however, that he must have mistaken three manatees for these fantasy creatures.

CARGO

At the time of Columbus, when ships embarked on voyages of exploration, they had to be completely self-sufficient for long periods at sea. Quadrants, compasses, and other pieces of navigational equipment were vital items. Copper cauldrons for cooking, candles, weapons, and goods, such as glass beads, hawks' bells, brass rings, and knitted caps, for bartering with any inhabitants of newly found lands formed an important part of a vessel's basic cargo. Live pigs and chickens, held in pens and coops, were kept for food, and some were slaughtered every day. Salted meat, dried fish, flour, rice, biscuits, chickpeas, lentils, beans, almonds, raisins, honey, cheese, olive oil, and vinegar were all stored below deck, together with medicines, firewood, powder for the guns, tools, buckets, spare canvas for the sails, charts, tools of many kinds, anchors, lanterns, harpoons, fishhooks, and rope, as well as casks of wine to keep the crew in a happy frame of mind. There were no fresh fruits or vegetables of any kind.

Compared to modern methods, fifteenth-century navigation was far from exact.

But Columbus also had other favorite methods of navigation, as he recorded in the log he made of the first of his four voyages.

> *Though all these things will be hard work, it is vital that I should not sleep but carefully watch my course.*
>
> COLUMBUS'S LOG, CONCERNING HIS FIRST VOYAGE

The crew used a method called "dead reckoning" to calculate the ship's speed. The pilot dropped overboard a weighted wooden plank attached to a line. Then, using an hourglass, the time it took for the ship to pass by the plank was noted. Combining this with the ship's known direction of travel as indicated by its compass gave them both speed and direction. They could mark the position of the ship on a sheepskin chart with the points of dividers.

LOGGING ON

Columbus was one of the first sea captains to keep a daily journal, or log, which he intended to present to King Ferdinand and Queen Isabella. As he wrote in the prologue: "I have it in mind to write down on this great journey with great care from day to day all that I may do and see and experience, as will hereafter be seen."

Columbus's log has proven to be a valuable historical document of life onboard ship. It shows that Columbus took his tasks seriously, especially when he was on watch. "I sleep very little when I am commanding the ship. I have to plot the course and take the speed and see that everything is properly recorded. I do not trust anyone else to do these things as should properly be done."

This decorative tile (*above*), from a monument in the Plaza de España in Seville, features Columbus repairing his fleet in the Canary Islands.

This tapestry (*above*) depicts Columbus's fleet with no crews in sight. In stormy weather, the men were needed on deck to prevent the ships from sinking.

At one point, Columbus even kept two logs — one for himself and one for the crew. He explained in his journal, "I decided at this point to reckon less than I made, so that if the voyage were a long one, the people would not be frightened and dismayed."

WHO DID WHAT?

Many tasks had to be carried out every day onboard ship, and a strict division of labor existed. The captain was responsible for running the ship, while the pilot and master were in charge of navigation and the crew. The boatswain looked after the sails and anchors and also had to kill rats. A steward supervised the food supplies, stores of water, and wine. Below deck, a caulker

manned the pumps and stopped the leaks. Three doctors, a cooper (who mended barrels), and a gunner also sailed with the fleet, as did a captain's page. An Arabic-speaking translator came along on the first voyage. As it turned out, there could not have been much for him to do.

Life onboard a ship of this time was by no means easy, and there might have been times when the entire crew paled with fear, clinging to the hope that a bird on the rigging or a crab in a net might be a sign they were nearing land.

Getting a good night's sleep was a problem, too. All the flat, covered space below deck was taken up by supplies, so the crew had to lie down wherever they could find a space. After the hard physical labor of running a sailing ship, they were probably too tired to care. Lookouts had to be posted, rigging needed to be adjusted, empty storage barrels were taken below, and fresh supplies were brought up from the sea in buckets.

Mealtimes were far from lavish affairs, and the crew subsisted on ship's biscuits and a little tough beef, pork, or fish with a pot of beans and portions of rice.

All this was prepared in

a shallow, sand-filled firebox. To make the meat more edible, the ship's boy would tread it for an hour in a barrel of water.

> *The voyage is growing long, we are far from home, and the men are beginning to complain about the length of the journey and about me for involving them in it.*
>
> COLUMBUS'S LOG, SEPTEMBER 16, 1492, SIX WEEKS AFTER SETTING SAIL ON THE FIRST VOYAGE

One of the more surprising aspects of Columbus's expeditions is that he set out to explore with such a small fleet. On his first voyage, he had only three modest vessels. Only ninety crew members manned the *Niña*, the *Pinta*, and the *Santa María*, which was both his flagship and the main cargo vessel. The size of the fleet, however, suited Columbus's needs very well at the time.

VARYING NUMBERS

On his other voyages, the number of ships varied according to how popular Columbus was with his sovereigns and how much faith they had in his work at the time. In illustration of this, after a triumphant return from his first voyage, his second voyage was far more grand. He commanded a fleet of seventeen ships carrying between one thousand and fifteen hundred people, including settlers, fortune hunters, missionaries, priests, and monks.

For his third voyage, which took two years to plan, Columbus had only six ships. For his fourth voyage, when he was fifty-one years old, he was only granted money for four small vessels. Such an independent man may have felt some frustration when faced with those restrictions. In spite of them, however, he remained determined to sail.

This woodcut shows Columbus taking leave of the Spanish sovereigns at the port of Palos in 1492.

When conditions at sea demanded their attention, the whole crew was called on deck to check the sails and the rigging.

DID YOU KNOW?

The Spanish crown decreed that all merchants supplying Columbus with timber and goods for his first voyage had to do so at reasonable prices and that he was not to be charged local taxes on whatever he bought to use onboard ship during the expedition.

WHERE IN THE WORLD?

As shown in this illustration (*below*), throughout new territories, over centuries, European explorers took Native people as slaves. Columbus was no exception to this form of exploitation.

Columbus spent weeks on end in unfamiliar waters, which could not have been easy. But an unswerving faith kept him determined to forge ahead.

It may be difficult to picture a world without many detailed maps, but in Columbus's time, no one had yet charted the entire globe. Mariners sailed using mostly guesswork. Indeed, few people in Europe then had any idea North America even existed.

Columbus's main aim was to find gold. To do so, he had to rely on information supplied by the Native people. He failed to find the huge quantities he had been led to expect were mined in the region.

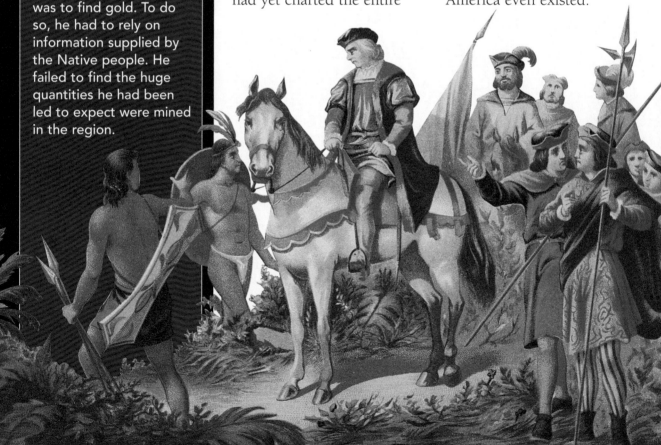

It is not difficult to imagine how exciting the prospect of landing must have been after many weeks at sea. Many members of Columbus's crew grew disillusioned by the dull routine of the voyage. How did their captain manage to encourage them to remain watchful? A silk jacket and a large sum of money provided by the Spanish sovereigns were promised to whoever sighted land first.

> **" The land appeared two hours after midnight, about two leagues away**
>
> Columbus's log, October 11, 1492 **"**

Columbus must certainly have thought they had reached the East Indies, because he called the Native people Indians. Still, when he did not find the cities of the Orient he expected, the prospect of exploring strange lands must have been daunting. No one could possibly have known what kinds of animals they might encounter or whether any Native people they met would be unwelcoming.

The arrival of Europeans

At one point on the first voyage, Columbus and his men thought they must be near land because they spotted what seemed to be large patches of green grass. They were entering the Sargasso Sea, an area with dense seaweed east of the Bahamas.

must have been equally startling for the so-called Indians. When they first saw Columbus and his crew, some of the friendly Tainos are reported to have shouted, "Come and see the men who have come from Heaven. Bring them food and drink."

The Tainos were a religious people, but their beliefs were very different from those of the Christian Europeans. They did not pray directly to their supreme deity, thought to be far too elevated to approach in this way. Instead, they relied on spirits known as zemis, who would help them in times of trouble. Small images of these spirits were worn around the people's necks, and larger effigies were placed in the chieftains' dwellings, where offerings were made to the zemis. Little evidence of local religious practices survives, however, because the explorers destroyed these idols.

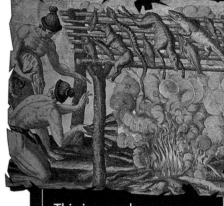

This image shows a method of cooking fish used by the Tainos of the Caribbean. The word "barbecue" is derived from their language.

Spanish explorers often forced Indians to carry their equipment, as shown (below) in this image.

MATTERS OF FAITH

Columbus was a deeply devout man, and every day at sea was punctuated not only by the watches (shifts) of the sailors, but by strict religious observance.

A page, for instance, began each morning with a chant that blessed God and also the day ahead. The Lord's Prayer followed, plus the *Ave María* and a nautical devotional:

"May God give us a fair day and a good voyage; may the vessels make a swift passage, with her captain, master and fine ship's company. May God give her a good voyage, and may God give you a good day, gentlemen, from stern to stern."

When sighting land after a long time at sea, the crew also routinely offered thanks by singing *Gloria in excelsis Deo,* which means "Glory be to God in the Heavens."

Fervent beliefs

Such was Columbus's personal faith that he wrote in his log after surviving a particularly bad storm: "I should have had less difficulty in withstanding this storm if I had only been in personal danger, since I know that I owe my life to my Supreme Creator and He has so many times before saved me when I have been near to death that actually to die would hardly have cost me greater suffering."

Columbus's zeal made him adamant in trying to convert all he met to Christianity. He wrote of the Native Americans: "They have no religion and I think that they would be very quickly Christianized."

In this respect, Columbus was acting in strict accordance with King Ferdinand and Queen Isabella's instructions to convert nonbelievers, Muslims, and Jews to the Catholic faith. Fifteenth-century Christian rulers felt they had the absolute right to win over heathen and infidel domains to their beliefs.

Columbus also wrote a so-called *Book of Prophecies.* This book was made up of passages from the Bible that were chosen to show that the discovery of new lands had been predicted. He also tried in vain to persuade Ferdinand and Isabella to undertake a crusade to the Holy Land.

In this painting, Salvador Dali tried to depict Columbus's conviction that he had been sent on a divine mission to find the New World.

This recent photograph was taken inside the Monastery of La Rábida, where Columbus once stayed.

When Columbus returned to Cádiz in June 1496 after his second voyage, he went to meet his royal patrons at the city of Burgos dressed in the habit of a friar, garb he is said to have continued wearing until the day he died as an outward sign of his religious fervor. He also turned to the friars of the monastery at La Rábida when, as a widower and before any of his major voyages, he was searching for a suitable environment within which his five-year-old son, Diego, might be cared for and educated.

This great explorer even believed at one stage that he might have found the garden of Eden. On his third voyage, landing at what is now Venezuela on the South American mainland, Columbus reached the conclusion that the place was so beautiful and blessed with such quantities of fresh water that he must have come across a terrestrial paradise. As he wrote, thinking he must have reached the Orient: "All the learned theologians agree that the earthly Eden is in the East."

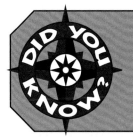

Columbus left on his first voyage with a document in Latin from the King and Queen stating that they were sending him to the Orient. He also carried three letters of introduction. One was addressed to the Great Khan, but the others were left blank to be filled in later as needed.

Columbus and his crew would have trudged through the same sort of landscape as is shown in this modern photograph of a forest river on the island of Guadeloupe.

Although the Tainos seem to have been meek, their accounts of other islanders known as Caribs must have terrified Columbus and his crew. According to the Tainos, they were "very enterprising since they come to all these islands and eat all the people they can capture."

GONE MISSING

A childhood friend of Columbus, Michele de Cuneo, wrote an account of Columbus's second voyage that describes the risks of venturing into previously unexplored territory.

"We landed on this island [Santa Maria de Guadalupe] and remained there for about six days. The reason for our long stay was that eleven of our men had formed a raiding party [to look for gold and plunder] and went five or six miles into the wilds, where they completely lost their bearings and could not return, even though all were seamen and observed carefully the position of the Sun.

"When the Lord Admiral [Columbus] found the men did not return and could not be traced, he dispatched two hundred men in four groups with trumpets, horns, and lanterns, but they could not locate them. There were times when we were more worried about losing the two hundred men than those they were seeking. But it pleased God to guide the two hundred, weary and hungry as they were, back to us. In the end we thought the eleven must have been eaten by Caribs. But after five or six days, it pleased God that, with hardly any hope of finding us, the eleven men lit a fire atop a rock. We saw this fire, sent a boat to them, and so they were saved."

Cuneo also reported rescuing from Caribs twelve girls and two boys, all about fifteen years old, who had been fattened up for a cannibal feast.

This photograph (*below*) shows a wooded part of the coastline of the island of Trinidad in the West Indies. Because it has three mountain peaks, Columbus named it after the Holy Trinity. Many of the names he gave to the places he visited had religious significance.

FRIENDS IN HIGH PLACES

Without the aid of King Ferdinand and Queen Isabella of Castile, Columbus might never have set sail on his voyages of discovery.

Columbus was to claim newly found lands for the Castilian sovereigns, whose coat of arms is shown here.

In 1486, the Royal Commission at Salamanca scoffed at Columbus for his ideas. He was so determined that he eventually won financial support for his attempts to reach the Orient by a new route.

Columbus was convinced God meant him to make important global discoveries, but others here on Earth also played a part in furthering the successes of his expeditions.

From the time he was a young man, Columbus was fortunate enough to have ready supporters. One of his brothers, Bartholomew, for example, though ten years younger, became a lifelong friend and fellow adventurer. When Columbus first arrived in Lisbon, Portugal, Bartholomew was already there. They combined forces to set up a mapmaking business. Later, Bartholomew approached both England and France to try to obtain the money they needed for the proposed first voyage.

He did not succeed, but Bartholomew was certainly an honest man, and there seems to have been no rivalry between the brothers. After Columbus had established the town of Isabela on the island of Hispaniola, he trusted Bartholomew to be left in charge while he returned to Spain. His youngest brother, Giacomo, later called Diego, also joined him on his second voyage. A cousin, Giovanni, captained a ship on Columbus's third voyage and later had the role of his aide.

FAMILY LIFE

Columbus was good looking by all accounts, but he had no money to speak of and few social or political connections. He married Felipa Perestrello y Moniz, the attractive daughter of a one-time governor of Porto Santo, a Portuguese possession in the Atlantic. She was related through her mother to the royal House of Braganza, and her father happened to be a renowned cartographer who had rediscovered Madeira and nearby islands, originally reached by Italian explorers in the fourteenth century. Felipa died young, shortly after their son Diego was born.

Some years after Felipa died, Columbus had a second son, Ferdinand, with Beatriz, the daughter of a peasant. He did not ever marry her, however. Some say that the reason was that after he became an Admiral, he regarded himself as socially superior. We do know that he recognized all he owed Beatriz because a specific addition to his will stated that she was to be provided for. He charged his first son, Diego, to see that the "mother of Don Ferdinand, my son, is given enough to live comfortably . . . because it weighs heavily on my soul."

GOOD SONS

The Admiral had very loyal children. Columbus's elder son, Diego, went on to become the governor of Hispaniola and married into royalty. Columbus wrote to him about Ferdinand, "Your brother, God be praised, is such a man that he will be very necessary to you."

Columbus's death was not marked by national mourning. His son Ferdinand wrote a fitting epitaph in his copy of a play, *Medea*, by the ancient Roman scholar Seneca. Ferdinand added a handwritten note to lines that foretell the discovery of new lands beyond a great ocean.

ALLIES OR FOES?

- The people of Palos, Spain, where Columbus was to sail, were ordered by Queen Isabella to equip the ships for his first voyage. They were far less impressed by him, however, than Queen Isabella was. They deemed his plan both foolhardy and dangerous.

- Martin Alonso Pinzón stepped in. A wealthy and well respected local seafarer, he had met Columbus at the Monastery of La Rábida. Pinzón succeeded in winning over the citizens and recruited sufficient crew in just ten weeks. Columbus was later betrayed by Pinzón, who abandoned Columbus's command and left in the *Pinta* to search for gold.

- Vicente Yanez Pinzón (*below*), the brother of Martin Alonso Pinzón, captained the *Niña*. He later found the mouth of the Amazon River.

This Spanish painting (*right*) shows Columbus and his son Diego with some of the monks at the Monastery of La Rábida shortly after Columbus's wife died. Without the help of these men of religion, Columbus would probably have had to forge a completely different career.

In this illustration (*below*), Columbus is discussing his plans with Father Marchena, a scholar and astronomer who was well known at the court of Castile.

The note reads: "This prophecy was fulfilled by my father . . . in the year 1492." His copy of the play is now kept in Seville Cathedral's Biblioteca Columbina, a library that houses a major collection of books from the Renaissance. Ferdinand assembled the original collection while he traveled through Europe.

BROTHERLY LOVE
Other "brothers" helped Columbus, too. They were monks who were not actually related to Columbus. When Columbus fled from Italy to Spain as a grieving widower with a young son, he was so poor that he had to beg for bread and water from the Monastery of La Rábida, near the town of Palos. The monks who lived there offered him far more than food. There he met sympathetic, scholarly individuals who understood what Columbus hoped to achieve and who even looked after young Diego while Columbus left for Castile to seek a backer.

A Florentine banker who was living in Seville proved enthusiastic about the enterprise and even offered to provide a few caravels.

This illustration (*right*) shows the monastery of La Rábida, where Columbus received shelter and sympathy.

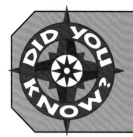

Queen Isabella is said to have spent so much money on the war against Granada that she had to pawn all her jewelry in order to finance Columbus's first voyage. Some historians think a certain Luis de Santangel eventually came up with some of the funding.

Columbus and his crew witnessed many customs of Native life. Here, Columbus is shown being crowned by a local chieftain.

ROYAL ASSENT

All this support was still not enough. Columbus needed money, so he had to persuade a wealthy and powerful sponsor to take a gamble on him. This meant he had to convince someone that there were riches to be made. He drew up a business plan and took it straight to the top.

First, he approached King John II of Portugal, who seriously considered Columbus's ideas. Later, however, the king decided Columbus was wrong and refused to sponsor the venture. Meanwhile, Columbus's brother Bartholomew asked for financial help from the courts of France and England. Both came to the same conclusion as the king of Portugal.

Columbus remained certain he was right, and his conviction grew until it became an obsession.

In 1489, King Ferdinand and Queen Isabella of Spain agreed to see Columbus. Although the queen was intrigued, Columbus's request was refused.

In 1492, however, the situation took a dramatic turn. The king and queen of Spain had finally crushed the hold of Islam in Granada and were feeling victorious. Queen Isabella remembered Columbus's determination to convert everyone he found to Christianity and recalled him to court. Sponsorship was settled when Spain agreed to finance Columbus's first expedition of three ships.

The Native people Columbus brought back to Castile after his first voyage must have been amazed by the Castilian court — and vice versa.

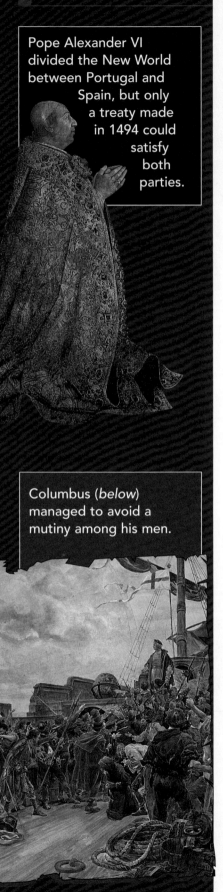

Pope Alexander VI divided the New World between Portugal and Spain, but only a treaty made in 1494 could satisfy both parties.

Columbus (*below*) managed to avoid a mutiny among his men.

MANY LUCKY BREAKS

Columbus faced countless obstacles — including shipwrecks, mutinies, and imprisonment — in his quest to discover a westerly route to Cathay.

Throughout his career, Columbus battled against an extraordinary variety of difficulties, from extreme poverty to dangerous encounters with hostile Native people, but he never despaired. Others around him were not so fortunate. Storms killed several members of his crew, and misfortunes hindered his enemies. Time and again, it seemed his luck was about to run out, but it never did. He became increasingly convinced he had been sent by God, while foes suspected he had evil powers.

Of all the fates that might befall a vessel, a shipwreck could be the worst. When this happened to Columbus, he managed to survive. Columbus left the helm of the *Santa María* at 11 P.M. on Christmas Eve, 1492, putting the entire crew in the hands of a young ship's boy. Then disaster struck. The vessel ran aground on a coral reef and was damaged beyond repair. Everyone had to abandon ship. Columbus might have given up at this point. He chose instead to see the situation as divine providence, or guidance from God. He wrote, "I recognised that our Lord has caused me to run aground at this place so that I might make a settlement here."

No hostile Native people emerged to take advantage of the vulnerable Europeans. The local people came out in force to help. They actually wept in sympathy for the shipwrecked Spanish sailors.

Columbus reassured his crew (*left*) about the distance they have sailed and the nearness of land. Meanwhile, he kept quiet about calculations he suspected might be more accurate in case these made his men even more anxious.

Their leader even presented the crew with two large houses in the middle of the village for temporary accommodations and gave them gold masks, jewelry, and solid nuggets.

> ❝ **We received such help . . . that [the ship] and decks were cleared in no time.** ❞
>
> COLUMBUS ON THE TAINOS' ASSISTANCE AFTER THE SHIPWRECK OF THE *SANTA MARÍA*

After a rather anxious Christmas, not knowing whether to stay or go on, Columbus decided to leave thirty-nine men on Hispaniola. They used the ship's remaining timbers to build a fortified settlement.

Columbus named this place Navidad (Spanish for Nativity). Thanks, he thought, to God's will, he had created the first significant Christian colony in the region.

Columbus managed to land on a few islands in the Caribbean, but it must have been entirely by accident because his maps were inadequate. He did not continue west. If he had, he might have reached Florida, the area of North America that was later discovered by Ponce de León, who was a member of the crew.

Columbus's ship, the *Santa María* (*below*), is shown as it is wrecked on a coral reef off Hispaniola. Nothing could be done to save the vessel, but the crew and helpful Native people managed to salvage the cargo.

Columbus had several physical problems. One of his illnesses may have saved his life and his crew. Pain and disability that may have been symptoms of arthritis were made more severe by bad weather and provided a warning that a storm approached so they were not taken by surprise.

The etchings of facial features on this rock are thought to have been made by the Tainos on the island Columbus named Santa María de Guadalupe, now known as Guadeloupe. No one knows the significance of the carvings.

This woodcut (*below*), illustrating a letter from Columbus about reaching the New World, shows a typical European view of Native people as cannibals.

Columbus tried hard to influence the Queen of Castile (*right*), with whom he had an audience in 1491. During this meeting, contrary to all previous indications, she agreed to give his proposal her full consideration. She eventually approved his plan for a first voyage.

Instead, he turned southwest. As we now know, he reached the West Indies, not the Orient, as he had been hoping. Yet he remained otherwise convinced. What added fuel to this belief were complete but probably wishful misunderstandings.

When the local population of Guanahani (or San Salvador, probably one of the Bahamas) spoke of Cibao, one of their settlements, he thought it must have been their pronunciation of Cipangu, Marco Polo's name for Japan.

Another case of misunderstanding is said to have occurred when local Native people tried to explain that great wealth could be found in Cubanacan. Columbus interpreted this reference as the name of Kublai Khan, one of the former great rulers of the Orient, so he assumed he was near his destination.

COLONIAL UPRISINGS

Columbus's second colony, Isabela, which he established in 1494 on the south coast of Hispaniola, was a disaster for him, the colonists, and the Native people. The Spanish colonists were not farmers but soldiers and noblemen, and none of them intended to work the land themselves. Instead, they took the Native people as slaves. Many of them died from hard labor, and others went so far as to commit suicide.

The colonists were also constantly fighting among themselves. When Columbus punished one of them by having him thrown from the prison walls to his death, word got back to King Ferdinand and Queen Isabella that Columbus had delusions of unlimited power

> **Other storms have been seen but none so terrifying.**
>
> COLUMBUS OF HIS LAST VOYAGE

and personal grandeur and had even gone so far as to shed Spanish blood.

In 1500, a Spanish nobleman, Francisco de Bobadilla, was sent to the region to investigate and saw more bloodshed in the form of seven Spanish rebels hanging from gallows.

Five more executions had been planned. Bobadilla promptly arrested Columbus and his two brothers and sent them back to Spain in chains.

Columbus then went to stay at the Monastery of Las Cuevas in Seville, where he was accompanied by a jailer for two months before the King and Queen of Castile granted him an audience. Columbus never allowed his chains to be removed, and this may have saved him. The sight of Columbus in manacles was too much for Queen Isabella. She granted him another voyage and gave his expedition further financial backing.

Columbus's crew was a tight team who had only each other to rely on for survival while out on the ocean. On his fourth voyage,

Columbus and his crew were shipwrecked again.

SAVED ONCE MORE

This time, Columbus became stranded on the island of Jamaica, but he had another lucky escape. He feared that one day, when the fancy seized them, Native people might either set fire to the two damaged vessels in which he and his crew were living or cut off their supplies.

After trading a helmet and some clothes for a canoe, Columbus persuaded two of the ship's officers to sail for help. They added a mast and a sail and set out for Hispaniola, even though it was thought impossible to cross strong currents in such a small vessel.

The officers were captured by Native people, but they managed to escape. After two desperate attempts, they reached Santo Domingo on the island of Hispaniola, where they managed to charter a rickety caravel. Almost a year after they had left Jamaica, the two men returned to rescue their shipmates.

WEATHER REPORT

Columbus and his crew always feared the weather. As he wrote in a log entry: "Last night the wind worsened and the seas were terrifying, crossing us from both sides and so distressing the ship that she kept losing steerage way . . . I was forced to let her drift astern wherever the wind took her. . . .

"Early in the night we saw a marvellous bolt of fire fall from the sky into the sea about four or five leagues away. . . .

"These things are disturbing and depressing the men, who are interpreting them as signs that we have taken a dangerous course."

Yet at times, the weather was balmy, and the sea was so calm that they could enjoy a dip.

SUCCESSES AND FAILURES

Columbus gives thanks to God (*above*) as he lands at Watling Island, or San Salvador, one of the Bahamas, in 1492.

When Columbus landed at Guanahani, the local name for San Salvador, he thought he was at a group of islands north of Japan.

In addition to his tremendous achievements, Columbus made costly and vital mistakes that are difficult to understand today.

Even before Columbus and his crew sighted land on their first voyage, there was excitement onboard as the weary men threatened to mutiny, adamant about having ventured too far south for the Orient and refusing to go any further.

Columbus appealed to their sense of religious duty and promised them riches. He also reminded them that he was probably the only one who could navigate them home. This idea may have saved his life. Finally, they reached a compromise.

He promised the men that if they did not see China or Japan within the next two or three days, they could turn back. In his log, however, he wrote something rather different: "I will continue until I find them."

Columbus had an excellent measure of his men. As soon as land appeared on the horizon, it was assumed to be their intended destination. Any thoughts of mutiny quickly vanished as each member of the crew struggled to be the first to glimpse these shores and any Native inhabitants.

Columbus had read the journals of Marco Polo and thought he would find lands peopled by the highly advanced Oriental subjects of the Mongol emperor

> 66 *They love their neighbors as themselves, and their speech is as gentle and kindly as can be, always with a smile.* 99
>
> COLUMBUS'S JOURNAL, DECEMBER 25, 1492

known as the Great Khan. Instead, however, he found several tribes with simple lifestyles and vastly different attitudes toward strangers.

The first people they met when they landed at an island he called Fernandina were the smiling, peace-loving, naked Tainos, whom he mistakenly called *Los Indos* ("the people of India"). Columbus wrote, "They became so much our friends that it was a marvel. . . . With fifty men, you could subject everyone and make them do what you wished."

In view of his religious beliefs, it is hard to comprehend how Columbus could meet such generous, caring people who had no need for prisons or forts on their island and believe that they should be captured and used as slaves for his crew.

The Tainos were delighted by their brave new friends and innocently thought that the explorers would help them in their continual fight against the neighboring warlike cannibals, the Caribs. Opinions are divided as to whether the Caribs ate their captives because they believed their flesh would give them extra strength or because they just liked the taste of human meat, especially of fattened boys.

Columbus's orders from Ferdinand and Isabella were simply to convert and conquer. The Taino Indians numbered almost one million in 1494, but after just five years, about one hundred thousand Tainos had died of hardship through enforced slavery or had been killed when rebelling against their inhumane treatment.

Born the son of a weaver, Columbus was awarded the impressive hereditary title of Admiral of the Ocean Seas.

Columbus insisted that the world was round, so it was impossible to sail off the edge.

Many sorts of exotic foods previously unknown on the continent of Europe were discovered by Columbus and his men.

Columbus won the full support of King Ferdinand and Queen Isabella of Castile.

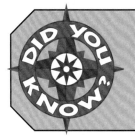

DID YOU KNOW?

The Tainos repeatedly told Columbus that if he wanted to find gold, he must sail south to the much larger island of Colba (now called Cuba) and Bofio (now known as Haiti and part of Hispaniola). Columbus looked in vain for signs of an Oriental civilization.

Within thirty years, they had been virtually wiped out.

ROYAL RECEPTION

Returning to Spain after his first voyage was undoubtedly the high point of Columbus's career. After years of ridicule, he had been proven right. He also brought evidence that he had been somewhere previously unknown to Europeans.

He traveled from La Rábida to Barcelona on horseback behind his precious cargo, which included parrots, pineapples, strange animals that had been stuffed, and six Tainos who were painted and wearing gold ornaments. The story goes that at every village he passed with this group, people turned out not only to stare but to cheer.

On April 30, 1493, he arrived in Barcelona, where he receive the highest honors at court.

> *The people are so kindly, and generous, and tractable and peaceful that I swear to Your Majesties that there are no better people in the world, and no better land.*
>
> COLUMBUS, SPEAKING OF THE TAINOS

Like a king, Columbus had his food tasted to make sure it had not been poisoned. He also rode in public next to King Ferdinand, which was an honor usually given only to other members of the royal family.

During his second voyage, Columbus engaged in a battle with Native people on Hispaniola (above).

When Columbus returned from his first voyage, he rode through the streets to cheers and jubilation.

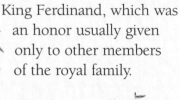

The disappointed Castilian sovereigns commanded Francisco Bobadilla to chain Columbus (*right*) and exile him from his colony on Hispaniola.

GENIUS OR LUCK?

By 1502, Columbus was no longer the governor of Hispaniola. That role had been given to Don Nicolás de Ovando. Ferdinand and Isabella had even forbidden Columbus to visit there on his fourth and final voyage. However, Columbus disobeyed them and set sail for the island that he had gained for Castile, noticing on his approach a higher tide than normal. Columbus knew that Ovando was about to send his fleet of thirty ships back to Castile and that these vessels were laden with treasure. Most of it had been stolen from the Indians, but some was Columbus's own share of the island's wealth.

Columbus sent one of his captains ashore to warn the new governor of a coming storm, but Ovando openly mocked him. Days later, the governor learned his lesson. Twenty-five of the ships went down. A religious man like Columbus may have believed that divine retribution was at work.

Columbus also had another lucky escape due to his quick thinking. On his fourth voyage, his ship ran aground on the island of Jamaica after another of the fleet had sunk. Columbus bought two Taino canoes and ordered two of his men to paddle to Hispaniola, which was a journey of more than one hundred miles.

For a whole year, Columbus was stuck on the island and reduced to trading for food instead of gold, with hawks' bells and sailors' caps. These goods no longer excited the natives, who refused to barter.

Columbus then came up with a plan to ensure respect from the Native people. Knowing there was about to be an eclipse of the moon, he told the Tainos that because his God was so angry, the moon would disappear. As it grew dark, all at once, the Tainos ran to get food for Columbus and his men, begging them to ask their God to restore the lunar light. Columbus's knowledge of astronomy had saved him and his crew from starvation.

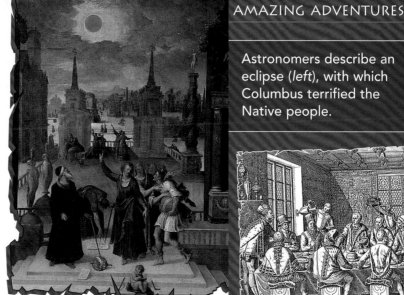

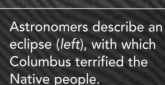

Astronomers describe an eclipse (*left*), with which Columbus terrified the Native people.

Columbus (*above*) demonstrates his theories on the shape and size of the globe with an egg.

Columbus is thought to have contracted malaria while in the West Indies. His brother Bartholomew took care of him.

The puffer fish is likely to have been one of the many bizarre creatures Columbus and his crew encountered.

WONDROUS NEW FINDS

The big-billed brown pelican would also have been an unfamiliar sight to fifteenth-century European adventurers.

Columbus did not discover the gold-roofed palaces described by Marco Polo for which he was searching, but he brought back many unusual and exciting items.

One native chieftain presented Columbus with a mask that may have looked like this South American one. The facial features were made of beaten gold.

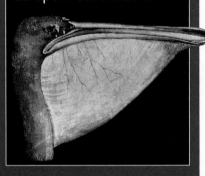

Gold was an obsession with Columbus and his crews from the beginning of their first journey, and they were intent on returning to Spain loaded down with it. At first, the natives seemed happy to oblige. Columbus wrote in a journal entry for December, 1492, "At sunrise the chieftain came to tell me that he had sent for gold and that before I leave he will cover me in it."

It was therefore hardly surprising that Columbus and his men soon became convinced there was an abundance of gold on the new islands they had reached. What was more, the natives kept assuring them that even more gold lay nearby.

"He [an Indian] told me that there is gold there in plenty, pointing to the caravel and saying that there were pieces of gold as big as the sterncastle."

Several times, Columbus was given masks of gold. At one point, his men even found quantities of gold lying in the sand.

Gradually, however, the demand for gold outstripped the supply. There were no mines, and in the Bahamas, the only gold lay in rivers.

PLACES OF INTEREST

Although Columbus never fully understood the significance of the islands he found, he renamed them all in the Spanish language after Christian saints or places and people that reminded him of his homeland.

Before Columbus's time, sailors slept wherever they could find a space below deck on their ships. When Columbus and his crew landed on an island in the Bahamas, they discovered that the Tainos relaxed in hammocks and adopted this sort of bed for life onboard.

Today, more than six hundred years later, we still have San Salvador (named after the Holy Savior), Trinidad (after the Holy Trinity), Hispaniola (meaning the Spanish Island), Guadeloupe (named after a monastery where Columbus had stayed), the island of Dominica (after his father), Santo Domingo (meaning Holy Sunday) on Hispaniola, and the Caribbean Sea, named after the Caribs.

FABULOUS FOODS

Columbus also fully expected to find a different source of financial gain as a result of his voyages of discovery — exotic foods that would make his country rich through trade — and he was right. When the captain of the *Pinta*, Martín Alonso Pinzón, came across rhubarb on the island of Amiga, Columbus sent a boat to fetch some.

The crew came back with only a single basketful, unable to get any more because of poor tools. Columbus wrote excitedly in his log, "I am keeping it to show your Majesties."

Maize (corn), potatoes, sweet potatoes, squash, kidney beans, tomatoes, peppers, pineapples, and sunflower seeds were all soon exported from the West Indies and became common parts of the diet of wealthy Europeans within one hundred years.

What the European explorers brought to the West Indies, however, was not so pleasant.

Large numbers of flying fish crashed into Columbus's ships in the Caribbean.

This splendid mosaic mask with teeth made from mussels is an example of the Aztec crafts found by the many conquistadors who left for the New World within a decade of the death of Columbus.

Columbus and his crew may have been surprised to find such curious vegetables and fruit as manioc (cassava) and bananas.

An iguana, spotted by Columbus and killed by his crew, was described as a serpent.

L. Flamineo

Columbus had probably never seen a flamingo (*above*) before visiting the islands now known as the West Indies.

Columbus's log contains several entries about seeing boobies (*below*) while at sea.

The sailors and later settlers introduced smallpox, measles, mumps, and whooping cough, illnesses to which the islands' population had no immunity. These diseases killed off a staggering 95 percent of the Native people. One nasty disease, syphilis, was spread by sexual contact between the Native people and Columbus's crews. The disease had lost most of its ability to overcome the local people's bodily defenses, but it was readily transmitted to Europeans.

Europeans also learned one very unhealthy habit from the island people. When they landed in Cuba, Columbus and his men were astonished to find the locals lighting one end of a rolled leaf and then inhaling the smoke through their nostrils. It was a curious procedure, but within a century, many people in Western Europe had become addicted to tobacco, with devastating effects on their health.

Columbus and his men learned not to be too rash in trying out new plants. On one occasion, they picked and ate some wild fruit only to find that soon after tasting it, their faces swelled and grew inflamed and almost unbearably painful. They treated the symptoms with cold compresses. This fruit is now believed to have been the manchineel, from which the Caribs made poison for their arrows.

NEW CREATURES

Columbus found the plumage of New World birds far more vibrant than those of Europe and their songs absolutely exquisite. There were even flocks of parrots so large that they darkened the sun. However, there seemed to be few mammals living on the lands he had reached, except for silent dogs.

A Dr. Chanca, one of Ferdinand and Isabella's physicians who was sent on Columbus's second expedition as ship's doctor and paid by them, even recorded in a letter to the city of Seville that, on Hispaniola, there were no wild beasts at all, "only a creature the size of a young rabbit, with a coat of the same kind and color. . . ."

It had "a long tail and hind and forefeet like those

> *They [the natives] live on bread made of the roots of a vegetable, which is halfway between a plant and a tree, and on 'age,' a turniplike fruit.*
>
> Dr. Chanca, ship's physician

of a rat. It climbs trees and many say the flesh is very good to eat.

"There are lots of small snakes but few lizards because the Indians consider them as great a delicacy as we do pheasants. . . . A very large lizard was seen many times and said to be as big as a calf and the length of a lance from tip to tail." This may have been an alligator.

Columbus also recorded seeing a seven-foot-long serpent (probably an iguana), which his men killed. Apparently, it jumped into a lagoon, and they had to chase it.

Columbus also recorded that "The men . . . also did some fishing with nets and caught large numbers of fish, including one just like a pig . . . but different from a tunny and shelled.

"The only soft parts are its eyes and tail, and a hole underneath through which it excretes. I am having it salted to bring to show Your Majesties."

In the waters around one unnamed island there were, according to Columbus, fish with the very brightest coloring, which provided his crew with much delight.

BELIEVE IT OR NOT

Some things that Columbus heard about from the Indians of the region, rather than experiencing for himself, must have seemed beyond belief to him.

He was told, for example, about a local tribe having the distinctive feature of a single eye in the middle of their foreheads. He was also told of an island where the natives were born with tails.

It was, of course, also a time of great discovery for the Native people Columbus met. They had never before seen such ships or people who went about fully clothed. But Columbus wrote that he deemed them intelligent and skilled navigators between the many islands.

A LASTING LEGACY

Convinced that he would be sure to gain a place in history as a result of his many discoveries, Columbus set about making a detailed record of his voyages for posterity. He had such a strong desire to be remembered and such a thirst for fame that when he feared his ship might sink, he wrote a brief account of his adventures and ordered it to be put into a barrel and cast to sea in the hope that it would be retrieved. Later, he also took it upon himself to compile *The Book of Privileges*, a collection of all the documents in which the sovereigns had promised him certain rights and titles. After Columbus's death, his son Ferdinand picked up the story and completed his father's biography. Together with Columbus's original log, these accounts left a detailed account of his four voyages.

WHO GOT THERE FIRST?

St. Brendan, who some claimed was the first to reach the east coast of North America, is seen here with a sea creature mistaken for a mermaid.

Accounts of St. Brendan's voyage were undoubtedly exaggerated. Here his ship is shown on the back of a whale.

Columbus is often called the first European to reach the New World. But several other adventurers may have been there long before he ever set sail.

By the time Columbus reached the New World, there had long been a Native population. The early inhabitants are believed to have entered the region as long as thirty thousand years ago, when they traveled from Siberia by way of Alaska across a land bridge that once existed where the Bering Strait is now. But there are many theories about who came to these regions thousands of years later.

THE NEWCOMERS

Some say that the earliest visitors to North America were Chinese or Japanese seafarers who landed on the west coast. They may have been fishermen who were blown off course from China or Japan. A piece of classical Chinese literature, dating from about 225 B.C., contains what appears to be an accurate description of the Grand Canyon.

SAINTLY APPROACH

A ninth-century chronicle, *Navigatio Brendani*, describes a voyage of St. Brendan.

One school of thought claims that Columbus was inspired by Viking legends when he traveled to Iceland on an early trading voyage. There he was told tales by the locals about the lands to the west as described by their Viking forefathers.

It tells how this sixth-century Irish monk claimed he found the Christian Utopia that he believed lay somewhere west of Ireland. It gives details of his adventures and states that he eventually reached "the promised land of the saints."

Some people believe St. Brendan crossed the Atlantic in a leather boat and reached the mainland of North America by way of Iceland. This version of events, however, is not supported by historical documents. Other people believe he landed on Madeira, a group of islands north of the Canary Islands. Others think he may have found the Canary Islands, which are northwest of Africa, and some believe he got as far as Greenland.

VIKING VOYAGES

Recent discoveries point to other settlers. In 1963, ruins of a Viking settlement were discovered at L'Anse aux Meadows on the northernmost tip of Newfoundland, Canada. Archaeologists identified six house sites and found a bronze pin, a fragment of bone needle, rusty nails, and a stone lamp. Radiocarbon dating of charcoal found in the remains of hearths shows the site was in use in about A. D. 1000. Two early fifteenth-century books confirm there were Viking settlements in this region. In the same area, tools and campgrounds of several other groups have also been found.

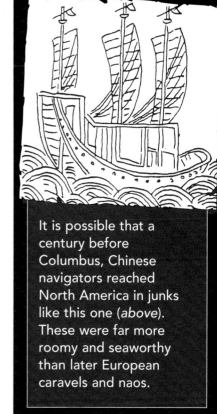

It is possible that a century before Columbus, Chinese navigators reached North America in junks like this one (*above*). These were far more roomy and seaworthy than later European caravels and naos.

This detail from a painting shows a triumphant Columbus disembarking on one of the islands of the West Indies. But was he the first to get there?

Mistaken about where he had actually landed, Columbus was still eager to exert his influence.

The Vikings of northern Europe had strong seagoing vessels and were skilled navigators. Historians believe they reached the New World long before Columbus.

Columbus used to sign his name (right) with words meaning "Christ-bearer."

> *There has been no such great-hearted man or keen navigator as the Admiral [Columbus]. He could tell from a cloud or a single star what direction to follow."*
>
> MICHELE DE CUNEO,
> SHIPMATE ON THE SECOND VOYAGE

Originally from Norway, a number of Vikings had been living in Norse colonies in Iceland and Greenland. From these regions, Leif Ericson traveled to North America.

There are several versions of how he got there. But the one accorded general recognition recounts that he had heard about the land from an Icelandic trader, Bjarni Herjulfsson.

Leif Ericson bought Herjulfsson's ship, sailed westward, and made three landfalls.

The first was at Helluland. Now known as Labrador, it was made up of barren rocks. The second, Markland (which may have been Newfoundland), was wooded with broad stretches of gleaming white sand.

The third, which he named Vinland (meaning Wineland) because of its wild grapes, is thought to have been in either Newfoundland or Cape Cod. The settlers only stayed for three winters. Then the lands across the Atlantic were forgotten for centuries.

Only a few years before Columbus sailed, the Portuguese made a number of attempts to cross the Atlantic. John Cabot's ship, the *Matthew*, is thought to have reached Newfoundland from Bristol, England, in 1497.

Columbus never reached the mainland of North America, but he visited Cuba, the West Indies, and Venezuela. He was an amazingly skilled mariner for his time, introducing — by accident rather than by design — European ways to a New World and vice versa. Such influences were not, however, entirely beneficial.

FOR FURTHER DISCUSSION

Many aspects of Christopher Columbus's life are thought to be controversial and therefore open to debate. The following questions can be used to guide classroom discussion.

1 Columbus was determined and persistent. How did these qualities help him? Did they ever work against him?

2 If you had to design a memorial plaque commemorating Columbus's achievements, what would it say?

3 Was Columbus popular with his crews? Would you have liked him?

4 What do you think Queen Isabella and King Ferdinand really thought of Columbus?

5 Columbus kept a secret log he did not show his crew. Do you think this was a good idea?

6 What aspects of Columbus's life show his religious fervor?

7 What kinds of new discoveries did Columbus and his crews bring back to Europe?

8 Do you think Columbus was a good father? Would you say his sons were loyal to him?

9 Who do you think helped Columbus the most?

10 Why is Columbus's log such an important document?

11 Can you list any of the mistakes that Columbus made?

12 Why is it incorrect to credit Columbus with the discovery of North America?

13 Who first inspired Columbus to travel and how?

14 Do you think Columbus was right in trying to convert the people he met to Christianity?

15 North and South America were named after Amerigo Vespucci, who crossed the Atlantic in 1499. Leif Ericson and John Cabot, among others, are believed to have reached the Americas before him. What other names could have been given to the continents?

16 Would you have enjoyed sailing aboard a fifteenth-century vessel? What are the principal differences between Columbus's ships and oceangoing ships of today?

17 If Columbus were alive today, what sort of career do you think he would follow?

MAJOR WORLD EVENTS

Columbus was born at the time of the Renaissance, which lasted from the fourteenth to the sixteenth centuries. During this era, enormous strides were made throughout Europe in the fields of art and science as well as exploration.

Find out about some of these major world events (*right*) and judge how they may have affected Columbus's accomplishments.

■ **1405-1433** The Chinese seafarer Zheng He traveled all over the Far East and to the Persian Gulf and the east coast of Africa, exploring and trading. He commanded a fleet of more than sixty ships known as the Treasure Fleet.

■ **mid-1400s** Great Italian artists Fra Angelico, Piero della Francesca, and many others were at the peak of their careers.

■ **1452** Perhaps the greatest genius of all time was born — Leonardo da Vinci, famed for his enormous contributions to architecture, mathematics, engineering, and art.

■ **1453** Constantinople (now Istanbul) fell to the Ottoman Turks.

■ **1455** In Germany, Johann Gutenberg produced the first printed book, a Bible.

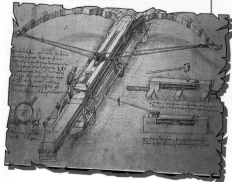

Leonardo da Vinci drew this ballista, or giant crossbow, a Roman weapon that he improved.

■ **1482-84** Diogo Cao of Portugal explored the African coast south of the equator.

■ **1497-98** Portuguese explorer Vasco da Gama led a European maritime expedition to India.

■ **1497** John Cabot sailed from England to Newfoundland, Canada.

■ **1499-1500** Amerigo Vespucci crossed the Atlantic and explored the Central and South American coasts for the Spanish and Portuguese crowns.

In 1492, the province of Granada surrendered to King Ferdinand and Queen Isabella of Castile after a ten-year war. Their attention then turned to sponsoring Columbus's voyages of discovery.

OVER THE YEARS

Christopher Columbus made four expeditions across the Atlantic Ocean looking for gold, spices, and a westerly route to Cathay. He reached lands previously unknown to Europeans, but he believed he had found the way to the Orient. He intended to gain converts to Christianity, but he caused much suffering and death for Native peoples.

Discover how some of his achievements have been remembered (*left*).

- A Columbus monument stands before Union Station in Washington, D.C., and looks directly across to the U.S. Capitol.

Columbus (*left*) was acclaimed an admiral and a viceroy by King Ferdinand and Queen Isabella, his royal sponsors.

- In 1812, a wilderness site was chosen for the state capital of Ohio and named Columbus.

- A Catholic priest founded the Knights of Columbus in 1882 in New Haven, Connecticut.

- More than thirty cities or towns in the United States share the seaman's name, as do many streets. The most famous is Columbus Avenue in Manhattan, New York.

- In Santo Domingo, the capital of the Dominican Republic, the Columbus memorial lighthouse was built in the shape of a huge cross. It opened in 1992. The light from its beams can be seen from miles away.

- The former King's College in New York City was renamed Columbia University in 1784 to acknowledge Columbus's pioneering spirit.

- In 1908, October 12 became known as Columbus Day in the United States.

- British Columbia, Canada, and the South American republic of Colombia are named after Columbus, as are the District of Columbia, the Columbia River in Oregon, and Colón, Panama.

- In a carved tomb in the Cathedral of Seville, Spain, is a casket that some people believe contains the remains of Christopher Columbus. First buried in Valladolid, they were moved to a monastery in Seville, then to Havana, Cuba, and then back to Seville again.

- The Christopher Columbus Awards offer middle-school students an opportunity to identify an issue they care about and develop an innovative solution using science and technology.

GLOSSARY

admiral: the supreme commander of a navy or a fleet of ships

amnesty: a pardon

astrolabe: an early scientific instrument used by sailors to navigate by the stars

astronomy: the study of the planets and the rest of the universe beyond Earth

boatswain: an officer responsible for the maintenance of a ship and its equipment

caravel: a two- or three-masted sailing ship used by the Spanish and Portuguese in the fifteenth and sixteenth centuries

Cathay: an ancient name for China

condemnation: a declaration of wrong or evil: blame

cosmology: the study of the nature and origin of our universe

crusade: a medieval European quest to capture the Holy Land and convert its inhabitants to Christianity

dead reckoning: the determination of the position of a ship without the aid of celestial observation by using a record of the course sailed, the distance sailed, and the amount of drift

dividers: an instrument for measuring or marking

domain: land under complete and absolute ownership

dowry: money or goods given to a husband by his wife's family at marriage

eclipse: the total or partial obscuring of one star, planet or other celestial body by another celestial body

effigy: an image or representation

emigration: the leaving of one's place of residence or country to live elsewhere

epitaph: a brief statement of remembrance for a person who has died

fanatic: someone who is obsessed by an idea or belief to the exclusion of anything else

fervor: intensity of feeling or expression

firebox: a large stove on a ship used for cooking food for the crew

flagship: the most important ship in a fleet, usually with the commander onboard

fleet: a group of ships under one commander

friar: a member of a religious order

gallows: a wooden structure once used for hanging people

heathen: an uncivilized or unconverted person

Hispaniola: an island in the Caribbean Sea, now divided into Haiti and the Dominican Republic

hourglass: a device for measuring time that has a glass vessel with two compartments. In one hour, a quantity of sand, water, or mercury drops from one half to the other.

infidel: someone who does not believe in a specified religion

Inquisition: a fifteenth-century tribunal or court of the Catholic Church that punished those not of the Christian faith, particularly Jews

Islam: the religion of the Muslims, founded by Mohammed

league: an old nautical measure of about 4.2 miles (6.8 kilometers)

log: a diary of daily events

malaria: a serious tropical disease

manacles: restraints or shackles for the hands or wrists: handcuffs

marooned: put ashore on a desolate island or coast and left to one's fate

master: the officer in charge of everyday matters on a ship

monastery: a home for people of a religious order, especially monks

Muslim: a follower of the religion of Islam

mutiny: a rebellion among a ship's crew

nao: a type of European cargo-carrying ship

nugget: a chunk

Orient: lands to the east of Europe

Ottoman: relating to a Turkish Empire, named after the Sultan, Osman I, who ruled from 1259-1326

page: a youth who attended a person of rank in medieval times

plunder: something taken by force, theft, or fraud: loot

prologue: introduction

prominence: something that stands out or projects beyond a surface

provisions: stock of needed materials or supplies, especially food

quadrant: an instrument used to aid navigation

Renaissance: a period of European history from the fourteenth to the sixteenth centuries during which there was a great revival of interest in art, literature, and learning

sovereign: a king or queen

sponsor: a financial backer

stern: the rear of a ship

sterncastle: a structure at the rear of a ship

steward: the person who organizes eating arrangements on a ship

viceroy: the governor of a colony or a country

FOR FURTHER STUDY

BOOKS

America in the Time of Columbus: From Earliest Times to 1590. Sally Senzell Isaacs (Heinemann Library)

Christopher Columbus. Peter and Connie Roop (Scholastic)

Christopher Columbus. Struan Reid (Heinemann Library)

Christopher Columbus: How He Did It. Charlotte and David Yue (Houghton Mifflin)

If You Were There in 1492. Barbara Brenner (Aladdin Paperbacks)

Pedro's Journal: A Voyage With Christopher Columbus August 3, 1492–February 14, 1493. Pam Conrad (Scholastic)

Where Do You Think You're Going, Christopher Columbus? Jean Fritz (Paper Star)

VIDEOS

Challenging Geography: Explorers Discover America. (Rainbow)

Christopher Columbus. (Schlessinger Media)

The New World Encountered. (Rainbow)

Spanish Explorers. (Schlessinger Media)

WEB SITES

Christopher Columbus.
www.nmm.ac.uk/site/request/setTemplate:singlecontent/contentTypeA/conWebDoc/contentId/137

Christopher Columbus: Extracts from Journal.
www.fordham.edu/halsall/source/columbus1.html

Columbus' letter to the King and Queen of Spain.
www.fordham.edu/halsall/source/columbus2.html

The Explorations of Christopher Columbus.
www.mariner.org/age/columbus.html

1492: An Ongoing Voyage.
www.ibiblio.org/expo/1492.exhibit/Intro.html